At the End of the Day and Other Poems

At the End of the Day and Other Poems

by

Christine Yurick

Cover design by Shay Culligan
Cover photograph by Christine Yurick
Author photograph by Michael Kahn

ISBN: 978-1-63980-177-0

Kelsay Books
502 South 1040 East, A-119
American Fork, Utah 84003
Kelsaybooks.com

To Michael, you were always the one

Acknowledgments

Grateful acknowledgment is given to the following journals and books where these poems originally appeared in the current or slightly modified versions.

823 on High: "Things These Hills Will Never Know"
American Arts Quarterly: "Hero Blames Leander"
Angle: "Self Portrait in an Olive Grove," "What Comes Out"
Autumn Sky Poetry Daily: "Borgau"
Autumn Sky Poetry: "The Ring"
Boxcar Poetry Review: "Claustrophobia"
East Coast Atlantic Beaches: "The Surfer"
E-Verse Radio: "Variation on an Old Saying"
Muse-Pie Press: "In Lucca"
Ocean Magazine: "Without Doors"
The Agonist: "Luggage," "The Figure in Your Photographs"
THINK: "He Said," "Before Coffee," "The Migration"
Tulane Review: "The Night Owl," "Answers"

Contents

Self Portrait in an Olive Grove

The clouds from the morning
have gone completely.
I sit in the driveway while
a man and a woman walk
toward the path next to the house.
Earlier, I watched you
walk through the olive trees.
It was cloudy then, and cold.
I know I am not very good
at waiting. The trees here,
they know all about waiting.

What Comes Out

Valdottavo, Italy

The sun is playing tricks
On the valley, but the stream
Doesn't mind, only I do
As I walk to the studio
To visit him, and he says,
What? You don't want
To write today?
And it made me feel
That same way
As when I run my bow
Over four strings,
Thinking that music
Will come out.

In Lucca

When they stayed in the house, they ate
Hearty meals and slept in every morning.
They looked at the town on the hill
But never went to see it. They complained
And rejoiced on different things. When
They opened their eyes and mouths,
What came in and went out they called art.
You even look Italian, he'd say to her,
Studying her nose. Sometimes she wore
A skirt and paced outside.

The Night Owl

No matter how hard I push the day on
it is still today. Though, on occasion,
when all is right in the world, I feel
like the night owl does when he hears
the clock tower ring and rejoices at the response
to the sound of its own voice.

Answers

Why does she stare at the window
with longing so often during the day,
asking questions without addressing
them to anyone or anything?
In the evening, he tells her that bed
is the best part of the day, and so
is the morning. But he doesn't know
how she plays in that big open room
which looks like her mind: clean,
orderly, everything put away.
There is a question in her eye
that does not dissolve when she sleeps.
There is a man standing outside.
When the clouds part, it is even warm.

Things These Hills Will Never Know

Valdottavo, Italy

No matter how far into the hills you go
there is another village. This one is wrapped
in fog, like the last village. The road
between them goes up, then down.
Narrow buildings stand along a creek.
The people here say words that are pleasing:
buon giorno, prego, grazie.
In Italian, nostalgia means
'homesick,' in Greek, 'a return home,'
in English, 'a wistful desire,
a sentimental longing.'
It is a trip to the coast after five days of rain
to see the cliffs, the rocks, the pressing waves.

Borgau

We are staying in that little apartment
above the pizzeria and have been roaming
the dry mountains like goats. It did not rain
for almost a month and we are both dark
from all of that sun and high from the fresh air
and lazy from all of the beauty.
The waves hit the brown-orange cliff.
The sheer blue curtain billows in the wind
brushing my cheek in the room where we make love.
The waves come in and go out again.

Paros

The storekeepers are returning from their siesta.
They unlock doors that are painted like the colors
Of the sea. There are muffled sounds coming
From the houses. An old man sings with a child
In a strangely beautiful language.

Another Country

One week ago, she was on the beach
in a blue skirt smiling at him
with his tan skin and blue eyes.
Now, she is standing in a doorway,
looking out as the fog settles
neatly into the valley and he is in the studio
working but it feels like he is in another country
and she is all alone. She turns on
the stove again, thinking of ways
to give him the things
she thinks he wants.

At the End of the Day

Every afternoon he walked
up the hill from the valley
to the stone house
where I was cooking dinner.
We would drink red wine
while he'd tell me about
his work at the studio
and I would read him
the poems I wrote,
even the bad ones,
which he thought
were the best.

Finally, something different

Kythnos, Greece

Everyone knows this secret,
they know that something different
is just what they need.

But, if they really knew this,
they would be like the retired Swiss couple
in the white house on the rocks
over-looking the goats and the sea
with their olive trees and the grapevines
and their warm, dark skin.

Before Coffee

In these quiet days, I forgive you
Because the rain comes and goes,
Because my body aches for your warmth,
Because you are different
And in the morning, you make me laugh,
Confusing me before I have had my coffee.

Acceptance

Early morning, shades of gray,
the sun laying color gently.
The trees in the valley are lush.
Shrubs on the mountain are dry.
They, like the grapevines and olive trees,
grow ancient in their dryness.
On the last day we walk
to the chapel overlooking the harbor
to sit in the shade. Every island has
roosters. I miss them now,
being further north and rainy.
They would crow all day and we
accepted that, along with the weather
about which they were always wrong, and our
captain to whom you could set your watch to noon
when he appeared from below with his grappa.

Claustrophobia

An abnormal fear of being in enclosed or narrow places

It's getting worse: strange bathrooms. Airplanes.
That bedroom in Italy with the bars across the window
And the door that stuck just slightly when you tried
To open it in the middle of the night. Elevators. Tunnels.
That hotel in Greece without door handles, the one
Where you place your key in a dish and it turns
On everything in the room. Movie theaters. Trains.
Like that cave on the Lebanese border where they
Showed us the tourist film. I thought, don't put me
In a cave and then shut the door. This is insane.
The cistern system under the city of David,
Where I saw the problem: you can't get in,
You can't get out. I thought I would die under there.
I only did it because we were with your family.
What I'm scared of: bathrooms. Getting stuck,
Of course, or not being able to get out, whatever is worse.
Oh, did I mention bathrooms? And the hotel with
The wall of windows over-looking an alley in Israel.
By far the worst was in that little tent in the mountains
While camping and the rain coming down in buckets.

You were always the one

There was stillness
and yet there was the rain
There was nothing
and yet it was blue
I have given up on worry again

I had given up my need
to control things
But it only really mattered
because I was there
and so were you.

You were always the one.

He Said

You have to look for the
distinguishing characteristics,
he says. The two masts,
the white sails, and the sea lavender
exposed at low tide. In the water,
he names boats: Joyant, Elena,
Mariquita. Right now, his back
is to me, hard and real. Spars,
spinnaker, jib. On land, he walks
around naming birds. Finch, crow,
chickadee. But I only see him,
eyes, hands, face. Then
again, eyes, hands, face.
I dream we will sail
to the shore, and he will
sing to me like the birds do.

The Apartment

The apartment had no address, it was too big
and the propane was empty, so we ate cold salads
after traveling to the island. I watched you drink
glasses of straight gin. I walked around half-naked
and at night we slept the sleep of hard labor and rough seas.
The rocky cliffs were ancient in their redness- leading
to small swatches of sand and emerald-blue water.
The Frenchmen were brass, slender and brown.
When the work was finished, we grew dark,
bought our daily baguette and drank wine until dawn.

Variation on an Old Saying

It was the year we fed the animals:
the birds, the possum, the brilliant fox
red against white snow. The winter
stretched on past April, past the fox
in the field, small against all that brown.
Days when the sky filled with birds
for miles. The hours I spent wondering how
I could ever go a night without you.
The long trips and dirty hotel rooms.
The Spanish moss dripping off the trees
like poetry. The sunny day on the dock.
The work. The pain at being with oneself.
It was the winter that you taught me
"One can never step into the same person twice."

The Path That Leads Does Not Return

You stand in the surf at dusk
And shyly watch the moon.
He turns to you, says,
'You think it moves, don't you?'

Silver water surrounds you
Pressing against your chest.
The colors in the sky
Are folding up and closing.
As if they had a choice.

You did not choose but still
You stayed the winter. You wonder
At the mind, at its slight fragility.
How some choices have no opposite.

Other Side

I am on the other side
of the once impassable mountain.
I arrived ravenous and transparent
as a west wind over still water.

Each Day

Each day the same cars gather and
the people smile and nod and stare.
The sun has risen over the inlet,
and the sparkles blind us. My love
is out there, battered by the wind, chasing
the sun. Near me, a woman laughs with her daughter.

There is a sureness to the ocean when calm,
like resting birds after their stubborn
persistence in flight. I wrestle with
these thoughts—memories of a cold night-
I look around. There are so many things
that I cannot name.

I cannot name the fire inside of me-
it is there on the plane, in my bed,
at the table, in my car.
It is a constant companion,
slow and steady, like the wick of a candle.

I'm here again; the people are gathering around me,
the ocean is sparkling, and I still have no names.
I look around and find that it is better to follow the wind
than fight it when all it does is blow.

The Words

Let me find again the words I used before
instead of love, like want, want as in
there is no other one but this. And need,
which is always there and not at all your fault
but certainly, you may try to fill it for a while.
The memory of your voice or the thought of your voice
the one I imagined before I met you
and I was reading your messages; I still
hear that voice sometimes and wonder why
your real voice sounds so different. You see,
I have expanded to fill the space between us
and now I cannot contract. Let's walk on this.
We will go past the spiderwebs filled with dew
and the bird song. See that flower over there
with the purple spike? It says we will weather
the years and change like snow. There is so much
that it knows that we do not know; it knows about
all the hours I will look out of a window waiting for you.

The Migration

You wait for the clouds to break,
And the sun to set. The hawks
Hunt the blooming dunes,
The yellow golden rod, dark clouds
Hold the sea like a blanket.
Sleep as dark as the black moon night.
Fog settles in over the creek. Waves
Resume their relentless pounding.
Fog fills in thick and fast, then leaves
Just as quickly. I want you to come
Back. You began your journey upwind
Then return at low tide. Migrating birds
Voice their journey overhead. They
Have been here before, and they will return again.

Without Doors

It is when the path spreads open
that the houses fall behind the dunes
and the sky bears the weight of openness
that the sea spreads out in front of me,
where the clouds are a high mountain
and the sun is a giant white ball, sparkling
on the deep sea, when the wild grass
surrounds my view, I realize that one comes
to the path so that they may live without doors.

To My Husband

I have been writing you
a love poem
for many years . . .

There are no words in it
and there is
no end to it.

Hero Blames Leander

Today, morning never arrived.
I sit and watch the sea
And know that darkening sky.

I stared and wondered why
The waves did rise
Wondered at this ebbing tide
And the anger in the sky
Without reason, without knowing why.

I stared and saw the waves were blue
And the waves were true.
Who had done them wrong?
Surely it wasn't I—
It must have been . . . you.

The Figure in Your Photographs

The figure in your photographs
is always walking away, so one can
only see the back. Or it appears as a small
dot, almost like an afterthought, in the center
of an exotic beach bathed in light.
Both of these facts make the figure appear
sexless—tall, lanky, broad shoulders, cropped hair.
Of course the figure is important,
to you or the art, else you would shoot it apart.
I like to think of the figure
as a random person who stopped so perfectly,
perhaps a stranger or a child
or a woman who stole your heart.

The Surfer

Low tide means a mile of what was underwater.
A few hours make the difference between a desert
with pine trees rising in mist and islands full of rock and waves.
It is the loudness of the surf that makes the quiet so great.

One surfer sits with his board. He stares at the sea.
What have you come for? the sea asks. *To master your power,*
the surfer replies. *And what do you know of my power,*
the moon intercedes. *Well,* the surfer hesitates,
then points at a seagull, *the seagull flies in the wind and dives
into your body to get its food,* he stops, then looks up at the clouds.
The bird doesn't think, and neither should I, the surfer says.
Then he smiles and rides the waves and is no more.

Hallways

It was never quite discussed,
Her interest in hallways.
What happened there, between
Two walls, a door at one end,
An opening at the other?
They never made it past that.
What was beyond those walls,
He wondered-
A bed? A kitchen, a couch
With a pair of pantyhose thrown across the back,
A pair of sandals on the floor,
A closet and clothes. A pet, perhaps.
A clock, a pair of sunglasses.
Tossed on the table by the door,
Her keys, a purse,
And her clothes scattered about,
Her there, kissing his neck.

The Ring

I want to stop that moment and live it again,
Only slower, your fingers grasping my hand.

You asked to see my ring; a stealth excuse
So subtly conceived; our hands were there now, level
With your desk, that picture of you and some *she*.
All I knew of you: a divorce, but now no ring.

Like the rays of light streaming in my window;
Arriving home my thoughts would not forget how
Your fingers grasped my hand. I could have taken
Off the ring, held it up for you to see.

Your mind and mine were level; you found an excuse
For that which we both desired but could
Not name, like the light breaking through my window,
That one should know its source through an object.

Like a simple ring, or the lack of one—
Wanted but not known, felt but withdrawn.

Luggage

for AS

I carry your love around
like a piece of luggage.
At the airport, it costs
twenty-five dollars to check it in.
I sit on the plane and doze off
knowing it is safe below.
When I get off the plane,
I pick it up again.
It is still intact.
But it feels lighter now—
had one of the carriers mangled it?
Did the flight attendant remove
something from it?
I shrug and walk on.
I carry it into my hotel room
and unpack it on the bed.
Skirts and shoes,
they are all here.
I lie down, put my feet up
look around and find
something is missing.

Philosophy of a Pretzel

There is only one mile between us.
The time it takes to travel that distance is insignificant.
It takes that long to fill your gas tank,
To sit at a traffic light while your eyes wander off
Where the clouds are like a symphony in the sky.
It is the amount of time it takes to break a heart.

There is a highway, traffic lights, trees, houses.
People live in those houses, and they watch
Behind green curtains. There is a detour.
I stop. I ask for directions. The people tell me
That the fastest route is around. In a circle.

The morning mist is a fog obscuring my direction.
The nights come, but the stars never rise.

Rejoice

I see women, like willows
long flowing limbs
effortless
I look at my body
tall wide hard with muscle
curvy

The wind is blowing
through the trees
the purple flowers rejoice

and, so do I.

Wild

I have lived a life your way
I have lived a life a different way
I have lived a life of talk
I have lived a life of silence
I have lived a life of indoors
I have lived a life of fresh air
I have lived a life of busy-ness
I have lived a life of stillness
I have lived a life of lies
I have lived a life of truth
I have lived a tamed life
I have lived a wild life.

I choose different and silence and air
I choose stillness and truth and wild.

About the Author

Christine Yurick is the founding editor of *Think Journal*. She has edited the books *Chester County Fiction* and *The New Cadet,* as well as the photography books: *Over the Dunes, East Coast Atlantic Beaches, Sailboats, Martha's Vineyard,* and *The Healing Power of Water,* all by Michael Kahn. Her poems have appeared in *E-Verse, Angle, American Arts Quarterly, Tulane Review,* and *823 on High,* among other journals.

www.ingramcontent.com/pod-product-compliance
Lightning Source LLC
Chambersburg PA
CBHW051434090426
42737CB00014B/2969